D0903119

-ink as in drink

Pam Scheunemann

Consulting Editor Monica Marx, M.A./Reading Specialist

Published by SandCastle™, an imprint of ABDO Publishing Company, 4940 Viking Drive, Edina, Minnesota 55435.

Printed in the United States.

Credits
Edited by: Pam Price
Curriculum Coordinator: Nancy Tuminelly
Cover and Interior Design and Production: Mighty Media
Photo Credits: BananaStock Ltd., Brand X Pictures, Comstock, Corbis Images, Hemera, ImageState, PhotoDisc, Rubberball Productions, Stockbyte

Library of Congress Cataloging-in-Publication Data

Scheunemann, Pam, 1955-
    -Ink as in drink / Pam Scheunemann.
      p. cm. -- (Word families. Set VI)
    Summary: Introduces, in brief text and illustrations, the use of the letter combination "ink" in such words as "drink," "pink," "shrink," and "wink."
    ISBN 1-59197-257-4
    1. Readers (Primary) [1. Vocabulary. 2. Reading.] I. Title.

PE1119 .S435158 2003
428.1--dc21   2002038205

SandCastle™ books are created by a professional team of educators, reading specialists, and content developers around five essential components that include phonemic awareness, phonics, vocabulary, text comprehension, and fluency. All books are written, reviewed, and leveled for guided reading, early intervention reading, and Accelerated Reader® programs and designed for use in shared, guided, and independent reading and writing activities to support a balanced approach to literacy instruction.

Let Us Know

After reading the book, SandCastle would like you to tell us your stories about reading. What is your favorite page? Was there something hard that you needed help with? Share the ups and downs of learning to read. We want to hear from you! To get posted on the ABDO Publishing Company Web site, send us e-mail at:

sandcastle@abdopub.com

SandCastle Level: Beginning

-ink Words

drink

ink

link

pink

skink

think

Roy gets milk to drink.

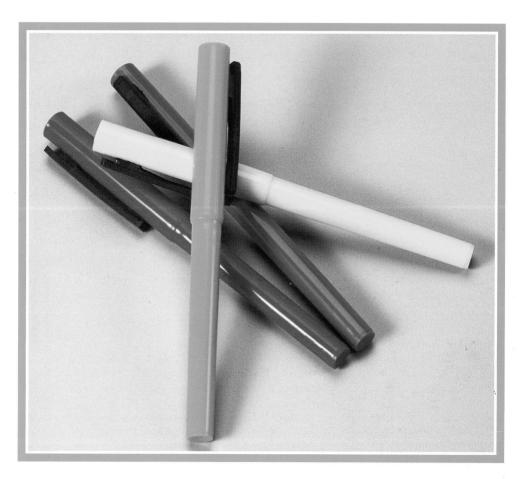

The pink pen has pink ink.

Joy, Erin, and Tracy link arms.

Dad is wearing a pink shirt.

A skink is a type of
lizard.

Jan likes to think.

Ernie the Giant Skink

Ernie was a giant skink.

He took a walk
to the skating rink.

Ernie passed by
some girls in pink.

He walked by Amy,
who was standing by a sink.

He also
passed
Mr. Fink.

Boy, did
his fish
stink.

He was hungry
so he ate a link.

After the link
he needed a drink.

Ernie finally came to
the skating rink.

As he stepped on the rink,
he began to shrink.

"Now I'm just the
right size, I think!"

The -ink Word Family

blink	pink
clink	rink
drink	shrink
ink	sink
kink	skink
link	stink
mink	think
Mr. Fink	wink

Glossary

Some of the words in this list may have more than one meaning. The meaning listed here reflects the way the word is used in the book.

ink   a colored liquid used for writing or printing

link   one of the rings that is part of a chain; to join together; one item from a series of connected items, such as sausage

shrink   to become smaller

skink   a lizard with a long body, smooth, shiny skin, and short legs

stink   to give off a strong, unpleasant smell

About SandCastle™

A professional team of educators, reading specialists, and content developers created the SandCastle™ series to support young readers as they develop reading skills and strategies and increase their general knowledge. The SandCastle™ series has four levels that correspond to early literacy development in young children. The levels are provided to help teachers and parents select the appropriate books for young readers.

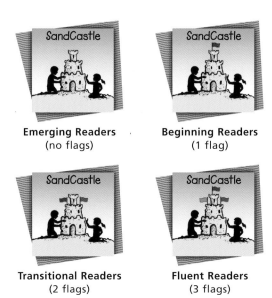

Emerging Readers
(no flags)

Beginning Readers
(1 flag)

Transitional Readers
(2 flags)

Fluent Readers
(3 flags)

These levels are meant only as a guide. All levels are subject to change.

ABDO
Publishing Company

To see a complete list of SandCastle™ books and other nonfiction titles from ABDO Publishing Company, visit **www.abdopub.com** or contact us at:

4940 Viking Drive, Edina, Minnesota 55435 • 1-800-800-1312 • fax: 1-952-831-1632